Your CAREER
DITCH IT
SWITCH IT

Here's How

Your CAREER DITCH IT SWITCH IT

Here's How

Dr. Shelly Cameron

Copyright ©2020

All rights reserved. No part of this publication may be reproduced, distributed, or transmitted in any form or by any means, including photocopying, recording, or other electronic or mechanical methods, without the prior written permission of the author or publisher, except in the case of brief quotations embodied in critical reviews and certain other noncommercial uses permitted by copyright law.

ISBN #978-0-578-77504-3

Library of Congress Cataloging in-Publication Data

Dr. Shelly Cameron

www.shellycameron.com

Request for permission to make copies of any part of this book can be made to www.shellycameron.com

First Printing 2020

Printed in United States of America

This book is dedicated to

Ashleigh-Ann

RJ, and Xavier

"With Every Success Comes Celebration"

Elaine Cameron-Walters

BOOKS AND PUBLICATIONS ALSO BY DR SHELLY CAMERON

The Leadership Challenge: Caribbean American Leaders in the United States
Published in Journal of American Academy of Business Cambridge (JAABC)

Success Strategies of Immigrant Leaders in the United States

Your Career: Ditch It. Switch It

My Safe Place

GreenLight: When God Says Go
Also available as Audiobook

GreenLight Journal

101+ Empowering Quotes For New Entrepreneurs

Motivational Quotes To Boost Your Success

Success Strategies Workbook

Success Strategies of Caribbean American Leaders in the United States

Success Strategies of Leaders

If you have not already done so, read the book "Success Strategies of Caribbean American Leaders in the United States" and learn the strategies on why some individuals succeed while others don't. It is now time to take the next step to do the work to become successful. *Ditch It. Switch It* is a How-To guide and provides exercises, activities, reflection questions, and personal assessments that are designed to help you take the personal learning journey to accomplish your dreams, goals, and aspirations.

Table of Contents

Introduction 1

Your CAREER DITCH IT SWITCH IT 7

Here's How 7

Self-Assessment Questions 10

Success 11

YOUR MISSION YOUR PATH 17

What Is Your Mission? 20

Goal Setting 23

Goals 26

LEADERSHIP DEVELOPMENT 35

The Leader in You 38

Leader at Work 43

Strategies for Dealing with a Bad Boss 45

SELF-MANAGEMENT 49

Self-Efficacy 52

Reevaluating Your Relationships 55

Self-Inventory and Taking Stock 72

CAREER MANAGEMENT 75

Taking Stock of Your Career 75

Rebuilding Your Career 78

How Can People Help You? 87

11 Rules of the Interview 89

Types of Interviews 90

Relocation 94

Resignation 97

Managing your Finances Establishing your Financial Management Plan 99
Repairing Credit 103
WORKSHEETS 107
Praise from Clients and Colleagues for the Author 119
Additional Offerings from The Author 121
About the Author 123

Introduction

Did I make the right choice when I was headhunted? Selena revealed that her 9-to-5 job was an exciting rollercoaster journey. Four years earlier, she was headhunted by a giant company to manage its flagship location. They had called her many times, but she avoided interview invites because of her job's loyalty. She was not sure how to tell them that she had landed a new opportunity. As time progressed, she went away to a distant country then returned to her home country, hoping that the headhunter would have forgotten, but they had not. On arrival back home, she was invited to an interview. This time she went. Not surprisingly, she was offered the job at twice the salary.

She was then faced with the predicament of telling her boss. When she did, she was offered promotions and many other perks. Still, she believed it was time. She moved on.

In another eyebrow-raising story, CNN Headline News told of a dramatic resignation by an airline representative who ditched his job in the middle of the Atlantic Ocean. When asked whether he had submitted a resignation letter, he said that he had not and did not intend to do so. Fed up, he basically told the airline to take its job and shove it.

Is that form of resignation acceptable? It certainly is, though the employer may request it in writing. I have seen resignations done in numerous forms throughout my career, ranging from the unbelievable post-it note on a supervisor's desk, the flight attendant who resigned on-flight, to the weather reporter who resigned while delivering her report on live tv. And of course, let us not forget the text message which would have made many cringe back-in-the-day.

No doubt, you too can share tales of similar drama when jumping ship. Suffice it to say; we fear change. We are uncertain how to tell our jobs that we must leave. Thoughts infuse our minds as we ponder whether we would be successful in a new environment. Will the perks be great? Will we get along with coworkers? Will we have to relocate? So many questions.

Then there are the misfits. They know they did not fit into the job from the beginning but stayed stuck with it because it paid the bills. So they live miserable every-single-day, year-after-year. Getting out of bed daily seems like a death sentence. Yet they stay trapped.

But sometimes we just simply have to ditch it! And yes, that is what this book is about. Ditch it Switch it, is for those who are miserable, stuck, dissatisfied, afraid, stressed, longing for personal growth or those who have a passion for entrepreneurship—a desire to build their own empire to leave a legacy. Yes, this book is for you, you, and you. This book will help you prepare to take the plunge. To launch out into the deep.

We always know when it is time to give up something. Our inner sense tugs if only we would listen. Often, we procrastinate, wondering if the feeling is real. Some stress it and get sick while others act like zombies.

Personally, I did that a few years. I loved my job—the pay, perks, the feeling of working with a giant international company that made a difference in people's lives. All were vastly satisfying for 14 years. But then the itch came that I could self-actualize and do more of what I wanted to do for others. But I stuck around for a few years after I got the itch. Later as I shared my story, an influencer described it as me leaving success to follow my dream, my purpose to help others self-actualize. When I finally made the leap, it was satisfaction guaranteed. But it took time.

But before you jump to do the same, there are things to be considered. I will share this through Forbes 14 Signs to know when it is time to Ditch your job as well as tidbits on resignation.

Signs It is Time to Ditch It or Switch It

Here are Forbes 14 signs to identify when it is time to leave your job.

1. You lack passion. That fired up feeling you had when you started
2. You are miserable every morning and dread going to work
3. Your company is sinking. There is no need to go down with a sinking ship
4. You really dislike the people you work with and/or your boss
5. You are consistently stressed, negative, and/or unhappy at work
6. Work-related stress is affecting your physical health outside the office
7. You do not believe in or fit with the corporate culture anymore
8. Your work performance is suffering. You are no longer productive
9. Your skills are not being tapped
10. You no longer have good work-life balance
11. You have been passed over for promotion or more challenging assignments
12. Your job duties have changed or increased, but your pay has not
13. Your ideas are not being heard
14. You are aware of or are experiencing sexual harassment or other illegal behavior

Reflect on these common signs that tell you when it is time to go, or if you need to switch careers. Seriously consider—can you picture yourself there in a year? A year is usually how long it takes for you to find a new and better job. It is not for you to jump ship at the first sign of discontent. Remember, you will always experience difficulty, crisis, or dull assignments no matter where you work. But it makes little sense to stay at a company because of inertia. As Jack Welch puts it, lock your door, and get out.

Resignation: A Few Tidbits

Many find themselves frustrated after turning in their resignations with immediate effect without thinking clearly about it. The next steps are filled with regrets and emotions about being emotional and angry. As an Organizational Development and Human Resource practitioner for over 20 years, I have had my share of employees who have acted in the heat of the moment; then later, we had to work together to clean up. So I caution you to think before you act. Understandably, you are frustrated. But are you adequately prepared for the next step in your career? Do you have up to 3-6 months savings to cover your bills while you job hunt or decide on your next step? How is your public profile? When employers conduct a search, what will they find? Educate yourself on life after your frustrating job.

If you experience negative feelings deep down in your gut in your attempt to answer these questions, then find a mentor or coach who can help you. Work with them to help you decide on the process of getting out of your comfort zone to do what you always wanted to do.

GOALS FOR THIS BOOK

This book is essentially designed as a key learning experience to help you on your journey to become more self-aware. As you engage in key reflections, it is anticipated that you will learn more about yourself and apply the skills necessary to drive your success. Therefore, the goal of this book is to help you to:

- Know when it is time to Ditch your job or Switch to a new Career

- Become motivated to Achieve your Goals

- Define what Success Means to you

- Reflect on what it looks like when you achieve it

- Build your self-awareness through understanding your Leadership Skills

- Take charge of your areas of development, including your life goals, career path and personal financial management skills

- Build your self-confidence

- Be so inspired that you experience change and share your success with others

In summary, success is no accident. You have to create it on purpose by taking specific steps. So get ready to succeed! Through your hard work, commitment, and dedication, you will succeed when others don't.

Your CAREER
DITCH IT
SWITCH IT
Here's How

The unexamined life is not worth living

-Socrates

Self-Assessment Questions

Achieving success starts with self-assessment. Briefly scan the questions below. As you begin this journey, you will be encouraged to consider and answer each question in detail as we progress throughout this book.

1. How do you define success and what does it look like for you?
2. What do you value most in life and why?
3. Are you where you want to be in life? if not, why?
4. How would you summarize yourself in fewer than two sentences?
5. What do you like least about your life?
6. Are you demonstrating the right actions, behaviors, and attitudes?
7. If not, what behavior and attitude adjustments do you need to make?
8. What are you most proud of?
9. What mistakes do you keep repeating?
10. What lessons have you learned in the past year? What lessons have you learned over the past 5 years?
11. What relationships are healthy for you and which ones are actually toxic?
12. What priorities do you need to shift?
13. What new skills do you need to learn?
14. What new goals do you have or will you set this year?
15. What additional education do you need to obtain?
16. What new career path do you need to take or what business do you need to start?
17. What resources do you need to leverage, and who else do you need to bring into your network in order to achieve success?

Success

Success is not an accident. We must create it on purpose by taking specific steps. In order to do that, we must first understand what it means. Have you given it much thought? What does success really mean to those who try so hard to get it, yet it moves further and further away as they draw near? Trying the short route, some play the lotto, anticipating overnight success. Some marry rich. Some scheme, connive, and conspire just to taste the mouthwatering trappings of success.

Without a doubt, few will argue that society's well-known individuals experienced success. Michael Jackson even produced an album 5 years after his death! Now, to many…that's success! But is it really?

Determined to find out why some individuals succeed while others don't, I decided to research the topic of success. I conducted a phenomenological study with Nova Southeastern University and interviewed outstanding leaders in business, healthcare, media, aviation, philanthropy and more. I even wrote books on Success Strategies and published a peer-reviewed article in the Journal of American Academy of Business Cambridge (JAABC) on Leadership and Success.

I also sought to educate myself not necessarily with the focus of being successful, since I already was—as I defined it. I went to college and earned several degrees, including two Master's and a Doctorate, combined with many years in International Business. Some would consider that I am successful as society envisions it. But is it really success?

That said, I implore you to plan to write your own definition of success. Decide how it will look when you achieve it. Will it be writing that first book that you longed for? Will it be Ditching that Career and Switching to a job that is more meaningful? Always remember that only you can define what success really means to you. Keep this in mind as you progress to writing down your goal(s).

That said, I have pulled together definitions from 21 of society's iconic leaders. Take a look. Reflect. Adopt one, and plan to write your own definition as we progress. Always remember that only you can define what success really means to you.

Definitions

1. Success is defined as the achievement of wealth, honors and the like (Dr. Fereshteh Amin).

2. Success is peace of mind, which is a direct result of self-satisfaction in knowing you did your best to become the best you are capable of becoming (John Wooden).

3. Success is going from failure to failure without losing enthusiasm (Winston Churchill).

4. Success is 1% inspiration, 99% perspiration (Thomas Edison).

5. Success is the result of perfection, hard work, learning from failure, loyalty, and persistence (Colin Powell).

6. Everyone can rise above their circumstances and achieve success if they are dedicated to and passionate about what they do. Do not judge me by my successes, judge me by how many times I fell down and got back up again (Nelson Mandela).

7. Try not to be a man of success, but rather try to become a man of value (Albert Einstein).

8. Eighty percent of success is showing up (Woody Allen).

9. The real test is not whether you avoid this failure, because you won't. It's whether you let it harden or shame you into inaction, or whether you learn from it; whether you choose to persevere (Maya Angelou).

10. We must accept finite disappointment, but never lose infinite hope (Martin Luther King, Jr.).

11. Don't limit yourself. Many people limit themselves to what they think they can do. You go as far as your mind lets you. What you believe, you can achieve (Mary Kay Ash).

12. Before anything else, preparation is the key to success (Alexander Graham Bell).

13. You don't have to be a genius or a visionary or even a college graduate to be successful. You just need a framework and a dream (Michael Dell).

14. The key to realizing a dream is to focus not on success but significance and then even the small steps and little victories along your path will take on greater meaning (Oprah Winfrey).

15. Always bear in mind that your own resolution to succeed is more important than any other (Abraham Lincoln).

16. Patience, persistence, and perspiration make an unbeatable combination for success (Napoleon Hill).

17. All you need in this life is ignorance and confidence; then success is sure (Mark Twain).

18. To love others as God loves you, that is the measure of success (Mother Teresa).

So there you have it: 18 of society's iconic leaders as they defined success. Look at them again…for a few times if necessary. Pause; reflect; adopt one or two and write it in the space below.

1) ……………………………………………………name of iconic leader.

Definition that has inspired you:

_____
_____
_____
_____

2) ………………………………………………… [name of iconic leader].

Definition that has inspired you.

_____
_____
_____
_____

SUCCESS: WHAT IT LOOKS LIKE

What does success look like to you? Take a moment and reflect. Take as long as you like. What is the image that comes to mind? In the space below, record it.

_____
_____
_____
_____

THE IMAGE

Now draw the image. Can't draw? No worries. Feel free to cut a picture and paste in an image unique to you. It can be a graduate, entrepreneur, marriage, family, or more.

YOUR DEFINITION

What is your definition of success? In the space below, write your own definition. If you already have a definition, review it. Redefine it if your thoughts have changed over time.

_____

_____

_____

_____

YOUR MISSION YOUR PATH

Every person above the ordinary has a certain mission that they are called to fulfill.

-Johann Wolfgang von Goethe

What Is Your Mission?

Now that you have defined what success means to you, it is now time to look at yourself and identify how you can be a better person. The first step is to find something that gives your life meaning. Here we consider our own personal mission. The late Steven Covey emphasized the stance to begin with the end in mind. It is the basis for making major, life-directing decisions, the basis of making daily decisions in the midst of the circumstances and emotions that affect our lives.

There are a number of things you can do. You can start by finding spiritual solace in your religion or in doing some of the things that you enjoy and find comforting. Why not look at life as having a lot more meaning? Perhaps the reason you are on this earth is to be kinder to other people, to make it a better world, as Michael Jackson sang, or to do something unique for others as Mother Teresa did.

Find out what your mission is and make a commitment to that mission. You may find that you do have a unique place in the world. You may even realize the importance of other aspects of your life.

When you are unhappy and experiencing self-pity, worrying about what is going wrong in your life, get up and take a look around. There are people who are in worse positions than you are. When you decide to look outside yourself, life takes on new meaning. Think about what you can offer to the world around you that no one else can. What difference can you make?

Here are some things you can do when the normalcy of life returns:

- Go to a hospital and hold a baby who is addicted to drugs

- Visit a patient who is dying of a dreaded disease

- Volunteer and read to the blind

- Adopt a pet from an animal shelter

Give of your time. Donating money to deduct from your taxes at the end of the year is good. But does it give you the added value of giving unselfishly to others? When you do good things for others, it comes back to you tenfold. So now it's time to do some introspection. The questions that follow will help.

- What is your mission?

_____
_____
_____
_____

- What do you really want to get out of life?

_____
_____
_____
_____

- Think of your ideal life. What does it look like?

_____
_____
_____
_____

- What do you value most in your life and why?

_____
_____
_____
_____

- What are you most proud of?

_____
_____
_____
_____

- What do you like least about your life?

_____
_____
_____
_____

- What mistakes do you keep making?

_____
_____
_____
_____

Goal Setting

To live a fulfilled life, we need to keep creating the "what is next", of our lives. Without dreams and goals there is no living, only merely existing."

- Mark Twain

Goals

Can you imagine setting a goal to climb Mount Kilimanjaro at age 84? Richard Byerley did just that! He was officially the oldest person to reach the summit of Kilimanjaro in 2011. Then in 2012, 85-year-old Martin Kafer and his wife Esther, 84, surpassed this goal. Not to be outdone, Angela Vorobeva reached the summit in 2015 at the age of 86 and in 2017, the new title went to Dr Fred Distelhorst, retired Orthodontist at age 88.

Naturally, these examples of goal achievement are no small feat. But what of athletes, professionals, scientists, and more? We all have goals. But what are they really? Are goals just a wish or a figment of our imagination of some ideal place that we want to be in the future? Think carefully. A goal is not a simple wish that you had a better car, a bigger house, a better job, a more profitable business, or a great vacation. Although it may begin with those thoughts, they are way too vague. Goals are so much more. Achieving your goal starts with understanding where you are, where you want to be, and how you intend to get there.

A goal is defined as the object of a person's ambition or effort, an aim or desired result.

Simply put, a goal is something that you are trying to do or achieve. Now that we know what goals are, let us consider why we should set them: simply because they give your life a sense of direction. Your goals must reflect your highest values, your mission—essentially, what you believe in. If you do not believe in something, then you will not do it. Take a moment and reflect on where you want your life to be, professionally and personally. See yourself doing what you dream. Make this a strong mental picture that will drive your actions.

In order to achieve your goals, you must take action. You must break it down into steps to achieve. If it is for your business—consider the type of business you want to be engaged in. How much should you be earning per day to get to your goal to become profitable? If it is to write your first book, how often should you engage in the writing process? Your goals must be concrete and clear. It is especially important to be clear. Spend time making sure your goal is clear. Enlist the help of a coach if you need help.

Write Down Your Goal

Take the time to think about the goals you want to achieve. Then write down your goal. Commit to them in writing. Writing down your goal is the first step to achieving it. It creates a contract with yourself to make your goals come true. Don't worry if the goal will take time. If you plan for it, you can do it. Don't be afraid to dream big! Dream the impossible!

My goals are:

1. _____

2. _____

3. _____

4. _____

Congratulations! You have already completed the first step to success. By setting goals, you create a map for your own destiny; you are acting on your life rather than simply reacting. Make the goals big and forceful! Something that will stretch you so that when you achieve it, you will feel completely satisfied. You may even motivate others!

Create a Plan

The next step in setting goals is to break them down into manageable, measurable parts. Let's say you set a goal for climbing Mount Kilimanjaro. The first thing you would do is organize the goal of the trek into small steps. Find out things like, where is it? How high is it? How do I get there? What is the best time of the year to climb? What guide company should I book with? How can I prepare physically? And so on.

Once you do your research, you will find that each small accomplishment will lead you closer to your goal. Once you have done all the preparations and you find yourself in the middle of the trek, exhausted and overwhelmed, this step-by-step thinking will help you stay on course and help you reach your goal to succeed.

Create a Deadline

Assign a realistic deadline to each component of your goal and write the deadline in your smart phone's calendar or whatever instrument you use. Tell someone you trust about your goal and deadline. Enlist a team if you think it will motivate you more. Doing so will further solidify your commitment.

Personal Goals Chart

Break your goals into manageable parts:

GOAL

1. _____

Step

a. _____

    Deadline: _____

Step

b. _____

    Deadline: _____

Step

c. _____

    Deadline: _____

Step

d. _____

    Deadline: _____

GOAL

2. _____

Step

a. _____

    Deadline: _____

Step

b. _____

    Deadline: _____

Step

c. _____

    Deadline: _____

Step

d. _____

    Deadline: _____

GOAL

3. _____

Step

a. _____

    Deadline: _____

Step

b. _____

    Deadline: _____

Step

c. _____

    Deadline: _____

Step

d. _____

    Deadline: _____

GOAL

4. _____

Step

a. _____

    Deadline: _____

Step

b. _____

    Deadline: _____

Step

c. _____

    Deadline: _____

Step

d. _____

    Deadline: _____

Continuously Act and Assess

Once that is done, you must review your goals daily. Look at them often so they stay on your mind. Don't worry about not making all your deadlines. If you miss a deadline, reassign another. Keep reassigning it until you complete it. Keep a positive attitude in order to make your dreams a reality.

PERSONAL GOAL CONTRACT

I, am setting a personal goal in order to help myself reformulate the following habit(s)/behavior(s):

The activities I plan to participate in will include

I agree to adhere to this structured program designed to meet personal needs for weeks. I will obligate myself to hours of the day toward the intended goal in order to increase my overall level of personal satisfaction.

I make this personal goal contract in order to achieve

_____

_____

_____

My incentive will be, which will be rewarded each day/week that I fulfilled my personal contract and came closer to achieving my goal.

Upon attainment of my goal, I plan to reward myself by

_____

_____

_____

Signed _____   Witness _____

Date _____   Date _____

LEADERSHIP DEVELOPMENT
DEVELOP THE LEADER IN YOU

Think Things Through
Then Follow Through

- Edward Rickenbacker

The Leader in You

What does being a leader have to do with you? You may say, I am not a leader, so this does not pertain to me. But reflect on your life: Are you a parent? Do you have responsibilities on the job? Are you a sibling? Are you part of an association, club, church, or other group? If you reflect on these, you will find that all these call for some form of leadership skills. At its inner core, we are responsible for leading ourselves.

We often wonder if success comes only to those individuals with certain traits or characteristics. Does it come to those who lead themselves and others? Good things come to those who seek them, not to those who wait for them. This was evident in a conversation I had at a conference with a talented middle-aged gentleman who had risen to the pinnacle of success in the performing arts. When I asked about his next step for his career transition (which he was concerned about), he shared that he is waiting on opportunities. Puzzled, I sought clarification. He explained that his work speaks for itself. I found it necessary to advise him that those days are long gone. No longer can individuals sit and wait on companies to call them for opportunities for which they may be qualified. In addition, with this age of rapid change in technologies, whatever made individuals like this gentleman successful before is no guarantee that it will happen again. Armed with internal traits, individuals must seek the opportunities, and more than likely, they will be successful.

The following sections highlight some of the essentials of leadership and the traits that can be seen.

Leadership Traits

Leadership is considered a trait. Each individual brings certain inherent qualities that influence the way he or she leads. Some leaders are confident, some are decisive, and others are outgoing and sociable.

Leadership is an ability. A person who has the capacity to lead is considered a leader. Leadership is also a skill that is conceptualized as a competency developed to accomplish a task effectively. Skilled leaders are competent people who know the means and methods for carrying out their responsibilities.

Leadership is also a behavior that is observable. When someone leads, that individual's leadership behavior becomes apparent, which means that we can see it clearly.

Leadership is a relationship that is centered on the communication and collaboration among leaders and followers rather than on the unique qualities of the leader. This means working with and through other people. A leader affects and is affected by followers. Both leaders and followers are affected, in turn, by the situation that surrounds them.

Positive traits. Positive leadership qualities include being trustworthy and just, foresighted, confident, intelligent, win-win problem solver, administratively skilled, excellence oriented, decisive, motivational, communicative, coordinator, honest, encouraging, dependable, team builder, and informed.

Another key attribute of leadership is the ability to *listen.* This is important even when the leader has to hear things that he or she does not want to hear. The leader must get the message even though history, anger, frustration, or hostility acts as a filter. Therefore, it is important to interpret the message to ensure mutual understanding.

Negative traits. Negative leader traits include being a loner, irritable, ruthless, antisocial, nonexplicit, dictatorial, uncooperative, and egocentric. The infamous Adolf Hitler is often referred to as the epitome of negative leadership. He has been described as determined to command personally. His behavior intrigued many and fell under what has been described as the psychodynamic leadership behavior. We will talk more about negative traits and bad behaviors as we progress later in this chapter.

Undoubtedly, we recognize that leadership is complex and includes many dimensions. For some, leadership is a trait or ability. For others, it is a skill or behavior; and for others, leadership is a relationship.

Top 15 Leadership Traits

Research conducted among industry leaders found that the traits they believed contributed to their success were self-confidence, self-discovery, values, vision, humility, commitment, persistence, optimism, family oriented, creativity, drive, learner, communication skills, passion, and responsibility. Below are Qualities of each. From the list select which ones you need to develop to enhance your own leadership style.

Leadership Trait	Description	Definitely Me	Need to Improve
Persistence	The desire to never give up in spite of all the odds.		
Self-Confidence	Includes a sense of self-esteem and self-assurance and the belief that one can make a difference. It allows the leader to feel assured that his or her attempts to influence are appropriate and right		
Self-Discovery	Pertains to an individual knowing his or her strengths, talents, and interests and what he or she can do well.		
Values/Ethics	Includes having true honesty and trustworthiness It provides a basis for understanding what it means to be a morally decent human being.		
Vision	Is identified by the ability to envision an uplifting and ennobling future, to have a dream or mission, to see the pattern, and to establish goals for oneself. Its growth is exemplified through studying, reading, comparing, traveling, seeing, imagining, seeking, and analyzing activities to create and receive views of what is possible.		

Humility	Typifies believing in good luck and possibilities beyond one's control, appreciating what life is giving, modest and willful, humble and fearless.		
Persistence	The desire to never give up despite the odds.		
Optimistic	Sees challenges as the beginning to a new success and willingness to tolerate frustration and delay with an optimistic outlook. An optimistic leader also has the drive to achieve, seeing an opportunity even in the face of setbacks or failure.		
Commitment	Is related to establishing challenges and expectations and applying oneself with focus and patience. The more difficult a goal, the more commitment is essential.		
Family Oriented	Is characterized by respecting family values and familial influence including mother, father, and extended family.		
Creativity	Involves being venturesome and originality in problem solving, thinking out of the box, and a multicultural problem-solving approach.		
Drive	This is the desire to do more and more and the determination to exercise initiative in social situations.		
Learner	Refers to the desire for lifelong learning and a consistent pursuit for knowledge.		
Communication	Being articulate, having people skills and listening skills, speaking publicly, and being able to communicate ideas. Verbally involved, informed, firm but not rigid, seeking others' opinions, and initiating new ideas.		
Passion	Defined by being passionate about what one is doing and putting one's heart into it, as well as connecting with the possibilities of the future and having the chance to do something about it.		

Change takes time and should be done through a step by step progress process.

Therefore, from the list of improvements that you identified, select the top three leader traits that you would like to work on in the next 30-60 days.

1. _____

   _____

   _____

2. _____

   _____

   _____

3. _____

   _____

   _____

4. _____

   _____

   _____

Leader at Work

We have all had to deal with bad bosses at one time or the other throughout our career. We scream, complain, lose the zing, become demotivated, do barely enough to get by, or inevitably jump ship. If you are dealing with a bad boss, here are a few examples of characteristics that depicts the behavior.

Common Bad Boss Behavior

1. Lack of vision and inability to communicate effectively
2. Micromanaging
3. Thinking you have all the answers and that you must have all the answers
4. Working late everyday
5. Poor hiring decisions
6. Fails to admit mistakes
7. Takes the credit but gives the blame
8. Does not lead by example
9. My way or the highway
10. Mistakes being liked for being respected
11. Provides little/no feedback or coaching
12. Shows favoritism
13. Task focused vs. team oriented
14. Embraces the status quo
15. Being a good doer means being a good manager
16. Selects and leads based on "like I do"

17. Ignores diversity of thought or varying opinions

18. Past focus vs. present/future

19. Lacks courage

20. Acts as a friend instead of a leader

21. Fails to delegate and demonstrate trust

22. Allows ego and pride to get in the way of good decisions

23. Has personal agendas/motives

If you are a new leader, reflect on these characteristics. Select the ones you need to improve and start working on it now. You will then be on your way to becoming a good leader.

1. _____

2. _____

3. _____

4. _____

Strategies for Dealing with a Bad Boss

Get angry! Tell them off on national TV like that famous weather reporter did! Give them a piece of your mind like that flight attendant did, then deplaned! Or quietly sneak away never to return again, which unfortunately happens too often.

Although we may smile at these examples, they are real-life situations that actually happened. As a HR consultant, I have worked with clients who have had these experiences and more. Because we spend most of our time at work, it would be great for us to really like what we do, and whom we have to work with.

Vincent Van Gogh said that he put his heart and soul into his work and lost his mind in the process. How many of us really feel that way? We show up every day doing a job that we don't like and then feel like we are losing our minds when we are expected to be productive and profitable. It's hard. But we keep at it if we are to cover our basic needs to survive and thrive, or for those at the higher levels, fulfill our higher need to self-actualize.

How to Manage

If you have a bad boss, it is not likely that you are going to change him or her. So here are a few strategies to help you take the steps to work better with a bad boss.

- Have an early, upfront conversation about what is important to you in a leader and how you can best work together. In a civilized manner, discuss things such as:

    - **Leadership style** and the coaching you would like to have to develop.

    - **Expectations**. What he/she expects from you, and what you expect.

- **Perception**. How each of you perceive "success" with regard to the job.

- What "meets expectations" or "exceeds expectations" look like on the **performance-rating** scale.

- Your current performance.

- Be proactive and check in with him or her often to provide reports or updates.

- Acknowledge them publicly for their support, especially when they have been instrumental in helping you succeed.

- If problems occur that escalate, have a conversation with the HR manager to ensure that any complaints are logged. HR will take the necessary steps to help resolve the issue and can serve as a mediator in future meetings.

- If 360-degree feedback systems and other anonymous options are in place in your organization, do use them to provide input regarding your concerns.

- Keep a record of dates, times, and specific examples of issues that have occurred so that you will be able to recall them when necessary.

- Essentially, do your best to try to work with the situation you are charged with at the moment. Nothing lasts forever. Things do change sometimes. But by all means, if the horizon really looks bleak in that company, then start the process to move on, especially if it starts to negatively affect your health. Start the job change process to search,

- Refresh your LinkedIn Profile.

- Create a personal website to share your experiences and achievement, especially if you are in the digital/creative industry

- Connect with a recruiter

- Consider other career options

It is important to use caution before you make such radical change. Making irrational decisions then saying "oh, wait" will be too late. So be cautioned that you *never leave a job without first finding another one*. It will be well worth it in the long run.

The actions that I will take to deal with my bad boss situation are:

1. _____

2. _____

3. _____

4. _____

SELF-MANAGEMENT

*Bulldozers move mountains;
ideas show where the bulldozers
should go to work.*

-Peter F. Drucker

Self-Efficacy

I dare you! Without hesitation she jumped off the cliff fully clad into the menacing waters below. "Way cool!!" her friends screamed, as she plunged safely.

Just think about that situation. How often do we act like that in our lives (well not to jump off a cliff which is a bit extreme), but do we dare to try new things? To step out; to take that leap that we are so afraid of?

Our tasks come and go day-in-day-out. Months pass and before we know it—years. We look back and realize that everything is different. Yet for many of us, things still remain the same. Our dreams, goals, entrepreneurial, and career aspirations remain at a standstill. We tremble at the sight of the raging waters below, afraid to jump!

On the flip side are those who step forward, take the leap, and discover triumphs they never knew existed! In order to be successful, you have to be motivated! And motivation comes from within! Enter **self-efficacy,** which means the belief an individual has in himself/herself to do things they never dreamed they could do. Essentially, self-efficacy reflects confidence in the ability to exert control over one's own motivation, behavior, and social environment.

Self-Efficacy reflects confidence in the ability to exert control over one's own motivation, behavior, and social environment.

Consider the descriptions of low and high attributes and check where you see yourself.

People with LOW Self-Efficacy

ATTRIBUTE (Low Self-Efficacy)	Yes	No
See challenges as threats		
Withdraw from difficult tasks		
Have lower aspirations		
Weaker commitment to goals		
Focus on limitations and failures		
Give up quickly in the face of challenges		

People with HIGH Self-Efficacy

ATTRIBUTE (High Self-Efficacy)	Yes	No
See challenges as goals to be mastered		
Set challenging goals and maintain commitment		
Sustain efforts in the face of failure in order to achieve		
Learn and grow from failures and try again—never give up		

Most if not all of us act in some capacity of leadership, be it in the workplace, or as a parent, teacher, or peer. In doing so we exert significant impact on those we have influence. Parents impact a child's self-efficacy (i.e. motivation) when they provide an environment that stimulates the child's curiosity and allows them to master their experiences.

A teacher's confidence in his/her own abilities to teach can impact how successful his/her students will be.

Peers model each other's experiences. She did it and therefore I can; or the converse, he did it and failed. Therefore, if I try, I too will also fail.

Our level of motivation is also influenced by how others see us. A coach's belief that you can totally do this or that drives the belief in yourself that yes you can totally do this.

Your personal physiological feelings also impact your motivation. If you fear public speaking, you become anxious and portray the belief that you are going to fail. On the other hand, if you feel anxious, but the anxiety does not show up as feelings of failure but feelings of excitement and achievement when you feel you are going to do well.

Drive your Motivation

Now take some time to think about your dreams, and the goals you set before. Are you where you want to be in life? Dig deep into your inner being and find that motivation... deep down because it exists. Bring it to the forefront of your mind. Start thinking positive thoughts like "*I can do this!*" Then look over the goal setting plans you made before. If you are off track and need help, connect with a mentor, or a friend who has your back, or get a coach. But whatever you do, don't let the next time you look back, you are standing still.

Reevaluating Your Relationships

Ever been around people who drain you? People who all they seem to do is focus on the dull side of life every single day? Then when you don't join them in their despair, they end up thinking you dislike them. Well sure since they drain every positive energy out of you.

Here are some signs of toxic relationships and people that you may recognize. Toxic people are those who are:

- Betraying
- Abusive
- Aggressive
- Bitchy
- Blaming
- Annoying
- Arrogant
- Ass-Kicking
- Bossy
- Backstabbing
- Blaming
- Defacing
- Dishonest
- Disrespectful
- Double-crossing

- Emotionless
- Exhausting
- Fake
- Fault-finding
- Hateful
- Hot-and-cold
- Hurtful
- Indifferent
- Irritating
- Intimidating
- Manipulative
- Judgmental
- Negative
- Narcissistic
- Obnoxious
- Phony
- Sarcastic
- Secretive
- Stingy
- Stubborn
- Skeptical

- Superficial
- Two-faced
- Victim-like
- Wishy-washy
- Worrisome
- Yelling
- Jealous
- Co-dependent
- Seeking to become a crutch
- Having ongoing drama and baggage in their lives
- Seeking to tear others down
- Don't dream big
- Are stagnant
- Are very negative
- Constantly rehash your past difficulties and tough times
- Do not like to see other people trying to improve their lives
- Make it a point to tell others what they cannot do
- Will not help someone take their life to the next level
- Cannot seem to keep a job
- Do not commit to anything
- Are constantly looking at the glass as being empty

The Toxic Terrors

Why does she always have to be mean? Why can't he understand? Why is it so hard for my boss to get it? Why does she have to always be so—toxic!

Yes, toxic. Indeed, it is a strong word which means pertaining to, affected with, or caused by a toxin, or poison. That is the meaning attributed to the word. Sad when it is used to describe an individual's behavior. But truth be told, there are many who act like toxins that poison our careers, dreams, goals, and aspirations. Year in and year out, time and again, they poison our ability to succeed. Yet why do so many choose to stick around such people? Toxic people are offensive, and people hate being around them. So in order to succeed, we must get away from them. It is difficult when you work directly with such individuals, but when you choose them as your good friends, it's a sure recipe for disaster.

Selected here are eight characteristics described by Dr. Lillian Glass, Expert in Human Behavior. As alluded, if you see yourself in any of the traits, don't panic! Simply recognize the trait(s) and start the process to do something about it. But first, brace yourselves and let's try to understand the various characteristics.

- **The Cut-You-Downer is:**

    - arrogant, mean, belittling, bitchy, hateful, self-righteous, condescending, threatened, superior, insecure, offensive, critical, sarcastic, disrespectful, underhanded, and fault-finding.

    - They have little self-esteem and will find fault with you and with everyone else. They love to belittle, taunt, ridicule, others. They cut others down so they can build themselves up.

- **The Self-Destroyer is:**

    - victim-like, unrealistic, weak, unstable, sabotaging, rejecting, negative, threatened, selfish, lifeless, desperate, unappreciative, depressed, defiant, rebellious, and out of control.

    - They hate themselves so much that they constantly tear themselves down and harp on what's wrong with them, while berating themselves. They usually say things like "I'm so stupid"; "that was dumb of me"; or "I'm the worst." In essence, self-destroyers try to cut themselves down before anyone else has a chance to do it. They hardly ever accept compliments and will negate any nice or kind words that come their way. They can be so full of self-loathing that they will become alcoholics, foodaholics, drug abusers, etc. Essentially self-destroyers don't think they are worthy of good things or deserve anything positive in life.

- **The Gossip is:**

    - Indiscreet, insecure, fault-finding, false, duplicitous, belittling, quick to place blame, brazen, clandestine, hypocritical, competitive, hurtful, self-righteous, shallow, sharp-tongued, skeptical, sneaky, imposing, adversarial, conspiratorial, critical, disloyal, meddling, mean-spirited, offensive, and angry.

- The gossip loves to spread stories even embellish them and may invent stories of his or her own. The gossip is usually a nosy person whose biggest pleasure is telling you about someone else's misfortunes. She might find pleasure in telling stories about others. Gossips generally have very little going on in their own lives. So they want to be accepted and to feel important so they bring you the latest news (real or imagined).

- **The Gloom-and-Doom Victim is:**

  - Masochistic, guilt-ridden, worrisome, sabotaging, resentful, rigid, selfish, rejecting, sad, negative, petty, fault-finding, paranoid, stubborn, whiny, weak, defeatist, unimaginative, self-destructive, fearful, solemn, cowardly, depressed, skeptical, unappreciative, suspicious, lifeless, lethargic, lackadaisical, defensive, and depressed.

  - Gloom and Doom victims are depressing to be around. Their energy really zaps you as they tell you how horrible life is, has been, and will be for them. They aim to make you feel sorry for them, but they have no interest in any advice you offer. Their preference is to wallow in self-pity, certain that the world has done them in and everybody has done them wrong. Nothing ever goes right for them. Maybe it's because their glass is always half empty rather than half full. They blame everyone but themselves when anything goes wrong in their lives.

- **The Opportunistic User is:**

  - Selfish, interfering, manipulative, back-stabbing, brown-nosing, secretive, indirect, disloyal, conspiratorial, dishonest, sneaky, unappreciative, underhanded, tenacious and seductive.

  - Opportunistic users are out for themselves alone. They are fair weather friends who want you in their life only when it is convenient for them—when they can benefit. These people will do anything to get ahead. If they can benefit from someone or have benefited all they can, they discard the person like a used paper towel, without a second thought.

- **The Me, Myself, and I Narcissist is:**

  - Selfish, egomaniacal, lacking in self-confidence, shallow, insecure, arrogant, boring, limited, socially inept, exhausting, obnoxious, flamboyant, self-centered, indiscreet, and a show-off.

  - They have only one thing in mind—themselves. They are the most self-centered individuals anyone can encounter; they don't want to talk about or do anything unless it pertains to them. They want to hear about your issues only if it affects them. Their vocabularies are over abundantly supplied with the words "me", "myself", and "I". Trying to have a conversation with a narcissist can be the most frustrating experience you will ever have, because they speak a monologue instead of a give-and-take dialogue.

- **The Competitor is:**

  - Provocative, fearless, fanatical, obnoxious, paranoid, offensive, pushy, aggressive, resentful, sabotaging, conniving, intense, intimated, defensive, confrontational, threatened, untrustworthy, negative, insecure, argumentative, and always looking for a fight.

  - Competitors seek every opportunity to outwit or surpass others. Everything is a competition from getting a job to getting a boyfriend or girlfriend, husband or wife. Competitors tend to be show-offs and braggarts who gloat about their achievements—both past and present. They constantly try to impress you with how much better they are than you. In essence they have such low self-esteem that the only way they can relate to you is by turning everything into a contest.

- **The Control Freak is:**

    - invasive, sabotaging, rigid, manipulative, arrogant, aggressive, forceful, backstabbing, self-righteous, meddlesome, confrontational, inflexible, egotistical, obstinate, pushy, unreasonable, stubborn, selfish, unaware, threatened, disrespectful, uncommunicative, and stubborn.

    - Control freaks can never let go. Like bullies, they are immobilized if not in control. However, unlike bullies, they don't always use anger or meanness to get what they want. Control freaks often use sweet talk and manipulation. They are not team players and have difficulty delegating authority, as they try to do everything themselves. If things don't go their way, they get angry or lose interest, for they feel they must always be in charge. Their lives are filled with frustration and disappointment, and never go with the flow. Instead, they force things to happen and when things don't go their rigid way they panic and become angry or more manipulative.

Techniques to Deal With Toxic People

The Cut-You-Downer:

- Handle with a calming questioning technique. Question in a non-accusatory manner and you will notice how the toxic behavior completely change for the better as he or she gets calmer and less hostile and even begins to smile when the truth is reached.

- When people have to cut you down it, is often because you have something they want or can't face. They feel inadequate around you. So give them the love-and-kindness technique. The focus on compassion makes it easier for you to deal with them.

The Self-Destroyer:

- Use tough love with the self-destroyer. Put your foot down and set limits. For example, "I will not marry you unless you stop smoking and drinking and get counseling."

- The other technique if all else fail (from above) then you may have to unplug and let the individual deal with the problem alone and in their own way. You can never help self-destroyers unless they are willing to help themselves.

As the saying goes, if you lie with dogs, you'll catch fleas. So if you hang out with a self-destroyer, you can be destroyed. Therefore, give them love and kindness, and if that fails, unplug.

The Gossip

- Gossips are extremely dangerous because they can make your life a living nightmare. So If they gossip with you, use the direct-confront technique and tell them their behavior is unacceptable if they gossip about you. If they gossip about someone you know or like, cut them off by saying I'm not going to listen to this or I don't believe a word of this, or I am not interested.

Use the humor technique with a comeback such as, "do you know what they did to people who gossiped in medieval times? They would put iron masks on their heads and lock them in with a key. Come to think of it, you would look pretty good in one of those masks. Maybe I can find one for you."

There is no room whatsoever for gossips in your professional life, as they can ruin your life's work. A gossip can destroy your business as fast as an arsonist destroys a forest with fire. Unplug!

The Gloom and Doom Victim

- The best technique with gloom and doom victims is tension-blowout. You need to blow out their energy repeatedly as it can be debilitating to be around them for a length of time. These people are like living negative mood contagions, and it may be very easy to catch their bad moods. Even if you give them the love and kindness technique, they are not going to believe you because of their feelings of total inadequacy. Therefore, if you value your sanity and you don't want to live a life of constant frustration, you have no choice but to unplug.

The Opportunistic User

- Use the direct confront approach which lets people know that you feel used and hurt by their actions. In some cases, confronting them will make the user feel bad or guilty about what they did. If your friendship or relationship means anything to them, users may take a second look at their behavior and how they have treated you. As long as it is done calmly, confronting them directly allows two people to begin to establish an open line of dialogue that could help in resolving any disturbed feelings.

- Sometimes you may use the direct-confront approach and the opportunistic user will deny or just not get it. When you know that the person is trying to use you or manipulate you in a situation, you have to say directly and bluntly, "no there's no way I am going to do that. I am not going to let anyone take advantage of me. The alternative is to unplug and never allow them to use you again.

The Me, Myself, and I Narcissist

- The me, myself, and I cannot speak any language unless it has to do with himself or herself. So use the "give them love and kindness" technique, because deep down, they are frightened, insecure, and underdeveloped human beings.

Understanding this may help you to become more sensitive to their needs and better able to deal with them. They are not necessarily trying to be selfish, they just are because they lack self-esteem. They can't give to others because they are depleted and empty as human beings with nothing there to give.

When their selfish ways and insensitivity become hurtful to you, you must speak up, using the direct-confrontation technique. However, employ a calm, controlled tone, otherwise they won't hear you. If you sound accusing or whiny, they will go on the defensive and either attack you verbally or deny that they are being selfish. Their egos are usually fragile.

- If you find that the narcissist makes time for you only when convenient, ignores what you say, and relates everything back to him or herself, you may want to question why you are around this person in the first place. You may want to unplug and be done with the Narcissist. Most people who deal with narcissists for any length of time will use the unplug technique because eventually their patience will run out.

The Competitor

- Use the direct-confrontation technique to tell the competitor that you are not trying to compete with him or her. If the competitor tries to top you, you might say, "I am glad you feel so good about yourself, but it isn't necessary to show off to let me know how much better you are. I am only trying to make conversation." Confronting the competitor directly often defuses the situation and lets the person see him or herself more clearly.

- Competitiveness is a sign of jealousy, which seeks to destroy everything and everyone. There's no way that you can have a meaningful relationship with anyone who is overcome with jealousy. It is in your best interest to unplug a personal relationship with anyone who persists in being competitive.

The Control Freak

- The control freak cannot function unless he or she is running the show. Children have a certain need to be controlled, but to adults with minds and values of their own, it is downright insulting and humiliating to be controlled by anyone. You have to set limits with control freaks. Let them know that it is their business if they are trying to control everything around them, but it is your business when they try to exert control over you. At the first inkling of controlling behavior, you must speak up, using the direct control technique. You can also use the mirror technique which will cause them to freak out as they immediately rebel against your attempts to control them. Apparently they really cannot abide what they do to others. Be aware that if you persist they will probably lash out at you verbally, with extreme vehemence. Eventually however, experiencing what it feels like to be told what to do and when and how to do it will usually deter their further attempts to control you.

- Relentless control freaks call for the "give them hell and yell" technique. Dig in your heels, push out your abdominal muscles and bellow that you will not be controlled or told what to do as you are responsible adult who can make your own decisions. Interspersing a bit of profanity may convince them of how angry you really are.

- If nothing works and the control freak continues to try to control you, leave you upset and frustrated, you need to unplug. Otherwise you will be assured of losing your identity and your ability to think for yourself.

In the list below, list your five closest friends and circle whether each relationship is Healthy or Toxic.

	CLOSEST FRIENDS	**STATE OF FRIENDSHIP**	
1		Healthy	Toxic
2		Healthy	Toxic
3		Healthy	Toxic
4		Healthy	Toxic
5		Healthy	Toxic

For those categorized as "healthy," are you leveraging and utilizing those relationships to help you become better? If so, how? If not, why?

_____

_____

_____

For those you circled as "Toxic," why are they in your life?

_____

_____

_____

How are those toxic relationships affecting you?

_____

_____

_____

Do you feel you attract toxic people? If yes, why do you think this is so?

_____

_____

_____

Sometimes we keep toxic people in our lives because we think that we can change or rehabilitate them. In reality, you will not be able to change them. It's a full-time job to change yourself.

Do you think you are a toxic person? Yes…………… No……………

If yes, what toxic behaviors do you display? Refer to the previously shown list.

_____

_____

_____

If you have identified yourself as a toxic person, focus first on yourself and make the needed changes. Negative and destructive thinking, language, and behavior will stifle your growth and the growth of those who are dear to you. There is much work to be done within before you focus externally.

What words do you use that may have a negative impact on others? Examples are:

- "You can't…."

_____

- "you aren't good enough"

_____

- "What were you thinking?"
  _____

- "I don't want to hear about this again"
  _____

- "You never…"
  _____

- "It will never work"
  _____

For each statement, write a phrase that would give the opposite message, a conveyance of encouragement or support. What else can you do to reverse your own toxic thinking, language, or behavior?

1. _____
2. _____
3. _____
4. _____

The Stress to Destress

In your efforts to achieve success, at times you may become stressed if there is a disconnect between your goal and its achievement. This is natural, as stress is something we all strive to avoid. But often, we find what seems like a *'stress to destress.'* We feel trapped, unhappy with our decision. But don't stress over it. Take baby steps. That's where most of us fall short. In our microwave society, we want to achieve our goals, dreams, and aspirations at the press of a button. Doing so is certain grounds for stress.

Here are things that people sometimes do to manage stress. Think back over the past month and check to show how often you have done each thing.

	ACTIVITY	REGULARLY	OCCASIONALLY	RARELY
1	Get plenty of rest at night?			
2	Talk about your feelings with friends and family members?			
3	Take breaks when doing difficult tasks?			
4	Drink fewer than three cups of coffee per day?			
5	Plan your time so that you could meet all your responsibilities?			
6	Use relaxation techniques?			
7	Ask others for help when you felt you had too much to do?			
8	Exercise?			
9	Talk about your problems with the people who were involved in them?			
10	Figure out whether or not you were feeling stressed?			
11	Find interesting things to do when you were bored?			
12	Plan time for relaxation?			
13	Look at the positive things in your life?			
14	Say 'no' to helping others when you felt you already had enough to do?			
15	Set realistic goals for yourself?			

Greenberg's personal stress profile recommends some easy to implement things you can do to manage stress better. These include:

- Taking care of your health, which means getting enough sleep, eat well, refrain from using drugs, and exercise regularly.

- Talk about your problems (stressors) with other people whose opinions you trust and with whom you feel comfortable sharing these concerns.

- Organize your time so you do not feel overly pressured, take breaks from stressful work, find interesting things to do as a diversion from your daily routine, focus on the positive actions of events rather than negative ones, and establish realistic goals so you are not frustrated by attempting to accomplish goals that are unobtainable.

It is also recommended that we accept what we cannot change, get organized, laugh at yourself, and definitely leave time for the unexpected. Those of us who are planners, often plan our tasks to the extreme leaving no room for the unexpected. This is certain grounds for stress.

Self-Inventory and Taking Stock

Selfie! Our society's phenomenon has made waves over the past few years! We take pictures of ourselves at home, at work, at play. We reach out to capture celebrities at public events and take that selfie to highlight our latest feat. It says we are cool. Way cool!

The drone and the GoPro make it even easier. With ease we can capture photos of ourselves in a crowd, at great heights on mountain tops, and even in the depths of the seas! The *Wall Street Journal* articles tell stories of injuries and even fatalities caused by this craze. *Narcissistic mentality*, they called it. Yup, these days we are filled with the craze! It is all about ourselves. But is it really?

To thine own self be true.

Self-Reflection

What about our inner desires? When was the last time you sat and took stock of where you are in life? Are you where you want to be? What are you most proud of? What do you like the least? Today, I encourage you to find some time alone to take stock of yourself.

Dr. Lillian Glass suggests looking at it mentally, emotionally, physically, and spiritually. As the saying goes—to thine own self be true. So be honest and assess yourself from your present situation to your ideal situation. Think of it as though there was nothing to stop you from achieving your dreams and making them a reality. Then list all the steps that you would need to take in order to make the dreams in your life situation come true.

For example, if you are single and wish to find a partner, at times you may feel lonely, empty, and sad. Your ideal situation may be to find a man/woman of your dreams—someone who speaks kindly to you and treats you with respect.

The steps to make this come true are:

- Tell your friends that you are available.

- Join a dating service, or a singles' organization.

- Give dinner parties and ask your friends to invite their friends.

- Go out more often.

- Get involved in classes or sports.

- Ask your minister or clergy for assistance.

- Be more open and friendly to people whom you meet.

- Be more assertive; smile and say hello.

Do Something Different!

Even though it is scary, and you may feel a little clumsy at first, do some things that you have never done before…yikes! Take trips by yourself; go to the movies alone; or have a cup of coffee solo. These things can build your self-confidence even if you are a bit nervous at first. You may also consider creating new adventures for yourself and doing things that are out of character. Get a new haircut, or a new color. Grow a beard. These will not only make your life much more exciting but also prevent you from feeling sorry for yourself.

In essence, it's about time. Step out. Take risks—and when you do, don't be afraid to feel silly, awkward, or of being rejected. Find comfort in the saying *"nothing ventured, nothing gained."*

The next page will help your self-reflection.

SELF INVENTORY REFLECTION

LIFE SITUATION	Present Situation	Ideal Situation	Steps to Achieve Ideal Situation
Social Life • Do you have enough friends? • Do you Socialize? • How often do you meet people?			
Work Life • What is happening on the job? • Is your salary sufficient to meet your needs?			
Professional Life • Evaluate the present status of your career. • Are you achieving your career goals?			
Family Life Consider the present status of your relationship with people who are close to you: children, parents, relatives, boy/girl-friend, husband or wife			
Physical Appearance Reflect on yourself from head to toe, including your weight to your speech.			

CAREER MANAGEMENT

Taking Stock of Your Career

In taking stock of ourselves, we should not forget that fear plays a large part in the drama of failure. That is the first thing to be dropped. Fear is a mental deficiency susceptible of correction, if taken in hand before it gains an ascendency over us.

-Douglas Fairbanks

Rebuilding Your Career

There is no such thing as a career anymore. The world of work now is much more fluid than it was in the past. Gone are the days of jobs for life where you did your time and left with a secure pension to enjoy retirement. You now need to take responsibility for your job security and career management. Make sure you discover and use your innermost resources and take a self-directing approach.

10 Key Points to Success

To accomplish this, it is necessary to keep reinventing yourself. Here are excerpts from Dr. Robert Davies' 10 key points to success:

1. Focus on your personal development. Spend some time thinking about the competencies —the knowledge, skills and abilities needed to survive in this era.

2. Always have a driving vision that consists of three components:

    - A clear mental picture of the person that you want to be;

    - A clear development agenda to help you get there;

    - A clear definition of the contribution you want to make to society.

3. Schedule a reinvention exercise for yourself every 3 years. Change with the times and avoid becoming obsolete.

4. Make a commitment to learn something notable each month. If you are not learning, something is wrong with the way you are managing your job and yourself.

5. Be concerned if you don't make any mistakes. This is not for you to go out and deliberately make mistakes. But if you are not making mistakes, you are not doing anything different. Treat failure as a learning experience and a platform to start a new chapter.

6. Never accept mainstream popular thinking without challenging it in your mind. Carve out time to challenge, research, and think differently.

7. Be confident. Never let anyone take that from you. But be quietly incompetent.

8. Keep an achievement diary. How has your work benefited others? Maintain an updated resume.

9. Invest in your network.

10. Help others. People are more than profit. Remember, there will be a time when you will also need help.

Personal Qualities of a Good Employee

Listed below are the soft skills most employers desire. Acquiring these skills will help you obtain the 'likeability' needed in finding and keeping your job. Include your soft skills in your interview answers and resume.

ATTRIBUTES	Yes	No	ATTRIBUTES	Yes	No
Dependable			Good at managing others		
Driven - passionate			Punctual		
Loves to learn			Flexible		
Can use language effectively			Good team player		
Goal Oriented			Good attitude		
Gets the job done			Self-Motivated		
Ability to multi-task			Energetic & Enthusiastic		
Good Problem Solver			Loyal		
Trainable			Adapt to change		
Values follow-up			Project Oriented		
Creative			Ability to identify opportunities, markets, trends		
Integrity / strong work ethics			Able to work with others and work independently		

Survey provided by Johns Hopkins University (through CareerSource)

Would you hire you? Why? Why not?

_____

_____

_____

_____

Be Prepared to answer these questions:

Are you a problem or a solution to a problem?

_____

_____

_____

_____

What kind of person are you?

_____

_____

_____

_____

What can you do well?

_____

_____

_____

_____

What distinguishes you from other people? Sell your accomplishments.

_____

_____

_____

_____

What would you hire you to do? (Be prepared to respond to job description based on the things you like to do and do well.)

_____

_____

_____

_____

Areas of Accomplishment

Often, individuals get stuck when asked the question about their accomplishments. Advanced preparation often helps in preparing resumes to show the difference or contribution you made to past companies. Be prepared to offer examples of accomplishments. The list below will help.

- Increased sales
- Increased profits
- Reduced overhead
- Increased inventory turns
- Reduced inventories
- Improved productivity
- Reduced overtime expenditures
- Reduced workforce/headcount
- Managed growth without additional costs
- Identified an overlooked problem
- Caught errors early
- Made your own job easier
- Overcame obstacles
- Met a difficult deadline
- Made job easier for others
- Implemented more efficient procedures

- Implemented new office systems
- Developed a training manual
- Trained new or existing employees
- Motivated employees to achieve goals
- Promoted employees
- Worked as production (office) team
- Suggested new products team leader
- Solved problems not related to my job
- Earned production bonus by exceeding quota
- Worked long and irregular hours
- Actively served on quality circle teams
- Eliminated costly downtime
- Reduced costly downtime
- Created new programs
- Reduced customer response delay time
- Evaluated new equipment
- Earned production bonus
- Promoted twice based on merit
- Retained existing customer
- Attracted new customers

Job Search

Things to Have/ purchase—job search tools (courtesy of CareerSource).

- An organized method to keep all your search activities and tracking forms
- A book/binder to hold your accomplishments, reference letters, and more
- Personal/legal pad and flap
- Smartphones and other methods to keep your contacts and schedules mobile
- Classy pen
- Thank you notes (for kind gestures)
- Stationery/envelopes for cover letters, resumes and reference sheets
- Professional interview and networking clothes and accessories
- Hairstyle and hair color, manicure
- Office, computer supplies, and postage

Things to Do Now

- Establish your LinkedIn profile, including a recent picture, recommendations, and endorsements.
- Prepare your Reference Sheet
    - 4-6 business, 2 personal references
    - Ask connections for LinkedIn recommendations
- Check your credit reports; go to www.annualcreditreport.com for a no-cost report.

- Fill in your binder with awards and recognitions, performance reviews, reference letters, notes/emails of appreciation from customers, vendors, suppliers, co-workers and community members. Show samples of your work.

- Establish your own website that highlights your work (e.g., www.weebly.com)

- Make a list of people in your network. Consider people you know from your work history, volunteer work, in your business/social organizations, school alumni, military and more. 80 percent of jobs are acquired through the help of other people. These are people you currently know, and/or do not yet know.

- Research online social networking sites to make new contacts and reconnect with your old contacts (e.g. LinkedIn, Twitter, and Facebook).

- Start practicing your interview answers and success stories.

- Tell your support systems that you are no longer available but now 'working' to find work! Set expectations.

How Can People Help You?

- Hire you

- Give you job leads

- Prioritize YOU, keeping YOU on their mind

- Refer you to specific openings

- Refer you to more contacts, directly or indirectly

- Give you company information

- Give you industry information

- Talk about trends/economic conditions

- Discuss specific jobs

- Discuss career paths

- Create an internship

- Critique your resume and cover letters

- Give you better job search strategies

- Recommend personnel agencies/recruiting firms/contract firms

- Talk about hiring practices

- Identify viable professional organizations

- Share their membership directories of targeted companies and contacts

- Suggest volunteer opportunities for exposure

- Offer information about:

- Conferences
  - Trade shows
  - Job fairs
  - Seminars
  - Short courses
  - Special events
  - Specific company based recruitments
- Clarify your marketing skills, strengths/weaknesses
- Be a reference, recommend/endorse you on LinkedIn
- Serve as your mentor
- Personally introduce you around
- Give you moral support/hugs and kicks
- Pass your resume onto others
- Provide local resource information
- Take you on a tour of their facility
- Offer you the opportunity to shadow them in their job
- Provide great websites, books, assessments and research material
- Validate you.

11 Rules of the Interview

1. Keep your answers brief and concise.

2. Unless you are asked to give more detail, limit your answers to 2-3 minutes per question. Record yourself and see how long it takes you to answer a question fully.

3. Include concrete, quantifiable data

4. Repeat your key strengths three times

5. Prepare five or more success stories

6. Put yourself on their team

7. Image is just as important as content

8. Ask questions

9. Maintain a conversational flow

10. Research the company, product lines, competitors, decision makers and other staff at the company

11. Keep an interview journal

Types of Interviews

SCREENING INTERVIEW/VIDEO INTERVIEWS

A member of the human resource department usually conducts the screening interview, which is meant to weed out unqualified candidates.

- Providing facts about your skill is important at this point.

- Interviewers use an outline of points they want to cover, looking for inconsistencies in your resume and challenging your qualifications.

- Provide answers to their questions but never volunteer additional information (which can work against you).

ONE-ON-ONE INTERVIEW

In a one-on-one interview, it has been established that you have the skills and education necessary for the position. The interviewer wants to see if you fit in with the company and how your skills will complement the rest of the department.

- Your goal is to establish rapport with the interviewer

- Show him/her that your qualifications will benefit the company

STRESS INTERVIEW

Stress interviews are a deliberate attempt to see how you handle yourself. The interviewer may be sarcastic or argumentative or may keep you waiting. Expect this to happen, and when it does do not take it personally. The interviewer may also lapse into silence during the questioning. Recognize this as an attempt to unnerve you. Sit silently until the interviewer resumes the questions. If a minute goes by, ask if he needs clarification of your last comments.

LUNCH OR DINNER INTERVIEW

The same rules apply as those held in the office. It is often used at the leadership level. The setting may be more casual, but remember, it is a business lunch, and you are being watched carefully. Use the lunch or dinner interview to develop common ground with your interviewer. Follow his or her lead in both selections of food and etiquette.

COMMITTEE OR PANEL INTERVIEW

Committee interviews are common practice. You will face several members of the company who have a say in whether you are hired. When answering questions from several people, speak directly to the person asking the question; it is not necessary to answer to the group. In some committee interviews, you may be asked to demonstrate your problem-solving skills. The committee will outline a situation and ask you to formulate a plan that deals with the problem. You do not have to come up with the ultimate solution. The interviewers are looking or how you apply your knowledge and skills to a real-life situation.

GROUP INTERVIEW

A group interview is designed to uncover the leadership potential of managers and employees who will be dealing with the public. The front-runner candidates are gathered together in an informal, discussion-type interview. A subject is introduced, and the interviewer will start the discussion. The goal of the group interview is to see how you interact with others and how you use your knowledge and reasoning powers to win others over. If you do well in the group interview, you can expect to be asked back for a more extensive interview.

Pre-interview Preparation

- Review your resume and be able to explain your job experiences, any gaps in employment, short job stints, and more.

- Engage in mock interviews. Find samples of mock interview questions at successfullleaders.net. Practice with friends, colleagues, or family members who will be able to help you with articulating clearly and concisely.

TIP: Practice providing your answers in fewer than 2-3 minutes per question. **INCLUDE:** What you did, what you learned, what you achieved, why it was important, and how that experience will help you add value to this organization (situation, task, action, result).

- Develop a list of questions to ask about the job or company. For example:

    - How would employees in the company describe the culture?

    - What are the three key challenges that the organization faces, and how are they addressing those challenges?

    - What resources or programs are in place to ensure that new employees are set up from Day 1 to be able to achieve success?

FACE-TO-FACE INTERVIEW

- This may be virtual and done online. If in person or online, show up ahead of time (15 minutes is good). If in person and you arrive earlier, sit in your car and wait.

- Sell and market yourself from the moment you walk in the door.

- Interact with everyone you encounter in a professional manner, whether it's the driver, the janitor, or elevator attendant—they may have key insights, and they may be able to provide the interviewer input regarding their impression of you.

- Greet the interviewer with a pleasant demeanor

DURING THE INTERVIEW

- Make eye contact.

- If asked, summarize yourself. For instance, the interview may say, "Tell me a little bit about yourself." Prepared elevator speech will come in handy here.

- Listen carefully to the questions being asked. Repeat them back or ask for clarification if necessary.

- Answer the questions in a clear, succinct way.

- Sell yourself, but do not overdo it.

- Ask your prepared questions.

- Explain why you feel you are the best candidate for the job. Your elevator speech is useful here as well.

- Let them know how important this role is to you, how interested you are, and how much you look forward to hearing back from them.

- Thank the interviewer for the interview invitation upon exiting.

POSTINTERVIEW

- Send a thank-you note within 24 hours to all the people who interviewed you. This may mean contacting the recruiter who set up the interview to obtain e-mail addresses. In the letter:

  - Thank interviewers for considering you for the opportunity and for their time

  - Emphasize that you are the best candidate and the right fit for their organization based on your skills and qualifications and what you learned about the job during the interview.

Relocation

Stay Focused. Go after your dreams and keep moving toward your goals.

~LL Cool J

What have I done? This is crazy!

A new job offer. Relocation. Tons of change. Excitement in the midst of fear. But it comes with the territory. Getting up and going to another land far away. Giving up the familiar is no small feat. Indeed it is scary—but you learn new things about yourself and others when you do it.

Moving From One Place To The Next

Have you ever watched HGTV's House Hunters International? Well, if you have, you will know that those who take on moving from one country or state to the next have brave hearts. They give up jobs, family, friends, and often wish they could take their home culture with them. Often, they must give up a lot to accommodate those fascinating new ventures.

We often say we want a change, yet we want to hold onto the familiar. It is normal. In my early career managing international HR, I had the task of sending executives to relocate overseas. It intrigued me so much that I studied Cross-Cultural Management. It was often a challenge for those who took the step. But those who embraced the host culture survived beyond the honeymoon stage. They became acclimated to the new culture filled with its languages, people, food, and new experiences.

It Works. Stick With It.

But like anything else, it works if we stick with it. Naturally, if you find yourself among those who do not like the experience after doing it, there is no problem. At least you can still say, "I did it"!

Only the adventurous can gleefully say, "what have I done? This is crazy!" with a smile and the satisfaction of new learnings and exposure.

5 Things To Do When Relocating for a Job

Relocation is a deeper dive than this book will offer, but it is a start because the decision is a serious one. Moving is one of the most stressful things to do. But moving for desired personal reasons, including a new job, new spouse (yikes!), education and more, makes the result more gratifying. We get that Adrenalin rush because it is something we desire. Packing those boxes, suitcases, and rummaging our belongings into trucks to go away, to relocate—makes the journey worthwhile (well, at least through the honeymoon stage). I have done my fair share and have also helped many transition their career to relocate in my HR consulting role.

To make things easier, Tor Constantino shared five things to ask for when relocating for a job. These are:

1. Take a scouting trip

    Purpose: To see your new home environment of course. Look for permanent housing while you are at it.

2. Ask About Temporary Housing

    This helps offset the burden of security deposits and helps in finding the best option for a more permanent home without the pressure.

3. Whole house pack and transport

    Some companies provide this, but it is cautioned to read the fine prints. Know what it entails and by the way, some things are tax-deductible. So save receipts for gas and more.

4. Storage of Home Goods

   Some transportation companies provide storage, which can be an advantage until you find your ideal home.

5. Cash Stipend for Miscellaneous Expenses

   And they do come in many forms, from airfares, car rental, family dislocation (some here, some there), and the like.

In summary, relocation is hard but sometimes it cannot be helped, especially when the grass seems greener on the other side. So get organized. Do not be scared but my personal philosophy is to do it afraid. Know that it is not such a bad thing. The more prepared you are, the faster you will transition and be settled into your new home.

Resignation

Many find themselves frustrated after turning in their resignations with immediate effect without thinking clearly about it. The next steps are filled with regrets and emotions about being emotional and angry. As an Organizational Development and Human Resource practitioner for over 20 years, I have had my share of employees who have acted in the heat of the moment; then later, we had to work together to clean up. So I caution you to think before you act. Understandably, you are frustrated. But are you adequately prepared for the next step in your career?

- Do you have up to 3-6 months savings to cover your bills while you job hunt or decide on your next step? How is your public profile?

- When employers conduct a search, what will they find? Educate yourself on life after your frustrating job.

If you experience negative feelings deep down in your gut in your attempt to answer these questions, then find a mentor or coach who can help you. Work with them to help you decide on the process of getting out of your comfort zone to do what you always wanted to do.

10 Tips to Resign Politely

If your response was positive here are 10 things courtesy of Huffington Post that you should do because resignation is the formal and final termination of your contract. So do it politely.

1. Talk to your manager or supervisor
2. Prepare a well-written resignation letter
3. Give your employer sufficient notice
4. Do not bad-mouth anyone

5. Finish all tasks

6. Do not post about it on Social Media

7. Offer assistance in the turnover process

8. Submit your resignation letter in person

9. Inform your colleagues

10. Show gratitude to the most influential

Managing your Finances Establishing your Financial Management Plan

Which of the steps below do you think are necessary to effectively manage your finances?

A. Step-by-step plan

B. Detailed financial goals

C. A weekly / monthly budget

D. The right resources

E. All of the above.

It is necessary to have all these steps in place, and more, to effectively manage your finances.

EXERCISE

To what extent do you currently have all of these in place?

Mark x in the appropriate column. The left side of the line represents not in place at all and the right side represents solidly in place. Where does each fall for you?

A Step by Step Plan						
Not in place		To some extent		Solidly in place	
Detailed Financial Goals						
Not in place		To some extent		Solidly in place	
A Weekly Monthly Budget						
Not in place		To some extent		Solidly in place	
The Right Resources						
Not place		To some extent		Solidly in place	

Examine your current financial status for the purpose of building a plan from scratch, reestablishing or refining your financial management strategy. Note that this exercise above is not meant to discourage you but to help illustrate where you should place your focus.

5 Steps to Financial Planning

In order to manage your personal financial plan, you need to do five things:

1. **Evaluate your financial health.** Start the process by taking a step back and keeping a log regarding on what you are spending money.

2. **Define your goal.** Identify what you are saving for and how much you need to save for things like retirement, or your child's education.

3. **Develop a plan of action.** Make spending conform to budget goals. But remember to life happens so be flexible. If something unexpected happens, make sure you are able to cover it.

4. **Implement your plan.** This is simple. Just start your plan now. Just do it!

5. **Review your plan.** Review your progress. Reevaluate and revise your plan. If things change, make sure your plan also changes.

Your financial management plan should be based on stable income. Your bills should not be based on money that you may or may not receive, such as on bonuses or commissions. Stable bills each month, such as utilities, car and insurance payments, groceries, rent or mortgage should all be based on your stable income. If you earn a commission but you have a base salary, then set your financial management plan to match your base salary. Your commission can be "discretionary income." If your job is mostly commission driven, determine your average commission over the last six months to a year or look at the minimum, and add it to your stable income.

Success coach Dr. Shirley Davis cautions that individuals must reconsider lending money to friends and family. Not only could it derail your efforts to get out of debt, but your friend or family member may not be able to repay you—and if you're expecting them to, it can impact your relationship. Instead, when you are able, give the money as a gift without the expectation of getting it back. For similar reasons, avoid cosigning loans.

Unexpected Bills

Inevitably, your future will include unexpected expenses. Set aside 10% of your net income into a savings account that you can easily liquidate in the event that you may need it.

Charitable Donations

Save another 10% for charitable contributions like tithes or offerings to your church or for a charity of your choice. This will also help with deductions when filing income taxes.

Automatic Deductions

Have money automatically taken out of your paychecks. You will not miss the money once you start to adjust your lifestyle.

Investments

Put your money to work. Invest in areas that yield dividends or interest.

Retirement Savings

Many employers offer a 401K match. For every dollar that you put into a 401K plan, they will match up to a certain percentage. The advantage here is that your contributions are deducted before taxes.

Tuition Reimbursement Programs

If you want to increase your value and enhance your resume with additional education and training, many companies will reimburse tuition expenses if you are gaining additional skills and knowledge related to your role in the organization. Also, take advantage of any special training your company provides onsite. Knowledge is power.

Group Life Insurance

Often, companies will automatically pay for one to two times your salary, and for a small premium addition, insurance can be added.

Holiday Shopping

The holidays are times when it is common to overspend. Make an effort to put aside an amount throughout the year. Then as the holidays approach, make a budget as to what you intend to spend, family and friends you intend to purchase a gift for, and the maximum amount you plan to spend. Try to take advantage of sales, purchase gifts in advance, and so forth, in order to save on the amount you budgeted. A Holiday Shopping Budget sheet is included in worksheets chapter.

Repairing Credit

Top 10 Tips for the Journey Toward Financial Freedom

Bad credit impacts most life decisions and goals. For that reason, Dr. Shirley Davis recommends 10 things to do to help you improve your situation.

1. **Know your current status.**

    - Use a budget spreadsheet to document your income and expenses. Include all income such as salary and child or spousal support and expenses such as utilities, phone, cable, internet, groceries, credit card payments, gasoline, car payments, etc.

    - Balance your budget to a zero balance. It is important that you account for every penny and that you decide what you are going to do with your surplus.

    - There are many free budget spreadsheets available. You may download one from www.successfulleaders.net. There are also budget spreadsheet templates in Microsoft Excel.

2. **Contact your creditors.**

    - If creditors are contacting you, confront the situation and take responsibility. Contact them as soon as possible and let them know your situation. Ask if you can work out a payment plan or request a deferral.

    - Many community organizations provide counseling and coaching free of charge.

    - You can do this on your own. Do NOT use a third party and spend money to have someone make a phone call you can make yourself.

    - Prior to making the call, know your interest rate, as it may be possible to have it lowered.

3. **Get copies of your credit reports.**

    - The law entitles you to one free credit report annually. Go to annualcreditreport.com.

    - You may benefit from setting up a monthly subscription for a minimal cost. This will help you track updates closely and on a timely basis.

    - Three credit reporting agencies—Equifax, TransUnion and Experian—will track your debt load, loan accounts and creditworthiness.

    - Obtain and review the reports for inaccuracies. Ensure that there are no unauthorized accounts and that all of your personal information is correct.

    - Request corrections by contacting the credit bureaus in which you found an error.

    - Find out your FICO score, which will rank between 300 and 900; the higher your credit score, the better rates you will get.

    - Know what impacts your credit score, for example, number of accounts, high balances, credit inquiries, late payments. Also, be aware of when credit inquiries are generated.

4. **Prioritize what bills you are going to pay down or pay off first.**

    - Determine the strategy that works best for you and your family. This may be to target high-interest accounts first, high balances, or small balances.

    - Paying off high-interest balances will save you money in the long run, but paying off smaller bills first will give you a sense of accomplishment and allow you to pay more on larger bills later. It's up to you. Just make sure you prioritize and have a plan in place.

- Pay off one credit card; then apply the extra money from no longer having that payment to double-up on paying off the next credit card, and so on.

5. **Set SMART goals.**

    - SMART goals: Specific, Measurable, Achievable, Realistic, and Time-bound.

    - For example: in the next 30 days, you will contact five creditors to set up financial arrangements.

6. **Make it a family affair.**

    - Get your spouse/partner involved and make this a teachable moment for your children. This could be a tough conversation, because money is very sensitive and sometimes controversial topic in a family; but make the commitment to have the conversation. Consider your family a part of the solution. Share with your children how they can be accountable for taking specific steps to help decrease the debt, for example, turning off the lights when leaving a room and the water when brushing teeth.

    - Allow your children to come up with a specific budget as well. If you give them a weekly or monthly allowance, have them come up with a simple budget. If you're giving them $10 a week, have them apply zero-balance budgeting and account for every penny. Get together on a monthly basis to check in on their progress and discuss improvements or updates.

7. **Conduct a quarterly review.**

    - This should be a formal review of your goals and current standing.

    - Conduct the review with your financial coach or accountability partner.

    - Make any necessary adjustments

    - Conduct this review every three months or at least semiannually.

8. **Journal your journey.**

    - Write down the lessons you are learning, actions you are taking, sacrifices you are making, the results and the impact you are seeing in your life.

    - Do this on a daily or at least weekly basis.

9. **Explore new avenues and new streams of income.**

    - Set up a plan to generate income above and beyond your current salary. Look for opportunities to leverage your gifts and skills into a backup pln.

    - Take a talent inventory. List the things you are really good at, that you believe can produce wealth. What is it that you can do better than anything else? What is in your mind that you can share and make money from it?

    - Refine your gift, and nurture it over time. The greater you develop the gift, the greater its marketability and, ultimately, the greater your income level.

10. **Celebrate and reward your successes.**

    - Document successes and reward yourself by treating yourself to something special.

    - Use good judgment and do not overdo it.

WORKSHEETS

Financial Management Plan Checklist

TASK		Due Date	Date Completed
	Document financial goals		
	Obtain a budget spreadsheet		
	Complete budget spreadsheet and achieve zero balance		
	Reduce expenses identified during budget development process		
	Contact creditors to work out a plan		
	Obtain and review credit report from Equifax		
	Obtain and review credit report from Experian		
	Obtain and review credit report from Transunion		
	Contact credit reporting agencies regarding errors		
	Obtain financial coach, mentor, or accountability partner		
	Prioritize pay-off and pay-down strategy		
	Develop goals and assign time frames. This sheet can help		
	Discuss and establish family accountability and goals		
	Determine financial plan review schedule and document it on a calendar		
	Document key milestones and planned celebrations		

Coach, Accountability Partner

_____

Expenses I Plan to ELIMINATE Immediately

Expenses I Plan to ELIMINATE Immediately			
Account or Expense	**Contact Information**	**$ Eliminated Monthly**	**Date**

Expenses I Plan to REDUCE Immediately			
Account or Expense	**Contact Information**	**$ Eliminated Monthly**	**Date**

CREDITORS TO CONTACT				
Account	Contact Number	Balance Owed/ Interest Rate	Agreement Made	Contact Name & Date

HOLIDAY SHOPPING BUDGET

Budget	Total Spent	Total Difference		
Name	Gift Idea	Budget	Actual Cost	Total
Mom	Scarf	$25	$20	-$5
Grand Totals		$25	$20	-$5

NOTES

NOTES

NOTES

NOTES

NOTES

NOTES

Praise from Clients and Colleagues for the Author

"Words alone can't express my gratitude and appreciation for the services provided by Dr. Shelly Cameron. In preparing for interviews I realized that I possessed the knowledge and skills necessary to perform my role as a healthcare professional. However, I lacked the confidence and ability to convey my worth to future employers. Under the coaching of Dr. Cameron, I was able to confidently and boldly stress how valuable of an asset I would be to future employers. Her strategies are thorough and effective. Thank you for providing me with the tools necessary to master any interview. –*Tamara Sawyers MSN/EDU,RN*

"I was one of your students in the workshop in the Professional Placement Network (PPN). I purchased your book and I enjoyed every page. Thanks for writing this book. I am very satisfied. I learned about Albert Einstein recovering from mistakes and it is important to remember that only the people that don't give up are the ones that succeed. Thanks again for your book. Waiting for the others" – *Milciades Adrion*

"It was a pleasure to meet you in your seminar. Thanks for sharing with us your experience. I admire your job and your charisma". – *Adriana Arias Restrepo*

"Great book by Dr. Shelly Cameron. Met her at the event dedicated to support Caribbean Entrepreneurs and more in (Washington) DC. Such a pleasure seeing someone who ascribes and embodies the ethos of her book. Success Strategies is a sweet source of regular inspiration and strategic direction that applies to my situation and that of many others. You can take a nugget at a time and apply that to an approach or predicament. Succeed and revisit for another nugget. Thank you for a great piece of work" – *Einsten Ntim, United Kingdom*

"I think success comes from achievement of a goal no matter how small. We are all successful but we have to acknowledge it and while we set ourselves new goals...we must not forget about our past successes while in pursuit of our latest target. When the journey seems hard that history of success is there to motivate us to go further" - *Gregory Turner, Author, Canada*

"We all have a purpose that we must accomplish"-*Pat Chin, Executive Director VP Records, NY*

Additional Offerings from The Author

Services Include:

- Keynote Speeches
- Leadership and Success Coaching (one-on-one and in small groups)
- Change Management Consulting
- Seminars/Workshops
- Online blogs (sign up at www.successfulleaders.net)

Most Requested Speaker Topics

- Your Career: Ditch It or Switch It
- 9 Steps to Writing Your First Book
- Bust the Fear! Find Your Heck-Yes!!
- The 5 Strategies to Managing Change for Women
- Follow the Leader, Leader. When Not To
- GreenLight: When God Says Go

CONTACT

Twitter: https://twitter.com/DrShellyC

Instagram: https://www.instagram.com/drshellyc_success/

Facebook: https://www.facebook.com/DrShellyCameron/?fref=ts

WORK WITH ME

Here are ways to learn from my knowledge and experience

1. **Search and Follow my Blog https://successfulleaders.net/**

   Find inspirations for success

2. **Subscribe to my updates**

   I write on Inspirations for Personal/Professional Development, Success, Management and Workplace Issues

3. **Buy my Books.**

   Read my Research titled **The Leadership Challenge** in The Journal of American Academy of Business Cambridge (JAABC). Books available on Amazon and www.shellycameron.com

4. **Book me as a Speaker.**

   I have been speaking publicly for over 15 years. I have given keynote, spoken at Events for Corporations, Nonprofits, Chambers of Commerce, Colleges, Clubs, Community events, and Churches. If you would like me to speak at your next event, please email me at scameron@ccahr.com.

5. **Hire me as your personal success coach.**

   I help Women Succeed in Business and in Life.

If you would like anything else, do not hesitate, contact me at scameron@ccahr.com. www.shellycameron.com

About the Author

Dr. Shelly Cameron is founder and managing Principal of Cameron Calder & Associates. She is a seasoned business consultant and coach. She specializes in the enhancement of performance management through helping organizations align their strategies, processes, and people.

Dr. Cameron is especially skilled in the healthcare industry, where she worked for over 20 years, including 14 years as Head of Human Resources for countries in the Northern Caribbean, with leadership in the Latin America region for the International Pharmaceutical giant, GlaxoSmithKline. She directed Leadership and Change Management initiatives during several international mergers, which culminated into the coveted Employer of Choice Award. She also managed strategic initiatives of medical clinics across South Florida, and over 17 boutique hotels in Fort Lauderdale. She served as Vice President for the Hospitality and Human Resource Association of Broward County, Florida (HHRABC) Board for over two years.

Dr. Cameron holds Doctorate in Education, major in Organizational Leadership, Masters Healthcare Administration, Master of Science in Human Resource Management, and Bachelors in Management Studies. She is a member of the Society for Human Resource Management (SHRM), HHRABC, and the Institute of Caribbean Studies in Washington DC.

On an individual basis, Dr. Cameron's mission is to connect individuals to their dreams, goals, passions, and aspirations. She helps overwhelmed high achievers get the clarity, confidence, and tools they need to succeed in business and life. A lover of dreams come through, she has helped many individuals move out of their comfort zones and into their passion.

At the community level through participation in workshops, health fairs and more, Dr. Cameron has collaborated with several organizations to contribute to the needy throughout the USA, Caribbean, and Kenya, East Africa. Her mission is to not only make a difference in the local community, but also to the wider society.

Through her book on Success Strategies of Caribbean American Leaders, Dr. Cameron revealed the results of a phenomenological study conducted with Nova Southeastern University and published in the Journal of American Academy of Business Cambridge (JAABC), which explored the hidden secrets of successful Caribbean American Leaders. She now connects it to those aspiring to achieve. Individuals are challenged to take that first step to accomplish their dreams, goals, and aspirations. As Author, Speaker, Coach and Human Resource Consultant, Dr. Cameron devotes her life to connect others to success.

For Speaking and Coaching needs, contact scameron@ccahr.com, or www.shellycameron.com.

www.ingramcontent.com/pod-product-compliance
Lightning Source LLC
Chambersburg PA
CBHW051149290426
44108CB00019B/2667